T0313640

The Bram Fischer Waltz

Harry Kalmer

The Bram Fischer Waltz

Harry Kalmer

WITS UNIVERSITY PRESS

Published in South Africa in 2016 by:
Wits University Press
1 Jan Smuts Avenue
Johannesburg 2001
www.witspress.co.za

ISBN: 978-1-86814-974-2 (Print)
ISBN: 978-1-77614-004-6 (PDF)
Also available in Afrikaans

Copyright © Harry Kalmer 2016
Foreword © George Bizos 2016
Afterword © Yvonne Malan 2016

Cover image © CuePix/Alexa Sedgwick. David Butler as Bram
Fischer in the production that premiered at the National Arts
Festival in Grahamstown, 2013.

Photograph of Bram Fischer © AAI Fotostock/Imago

All rights reserved. No part of this book may be reproduced, stored
in a retrieval system, or transmitted in any form or by any means,
electronic or mechanical, including photocopying, recording or
by any information storage and retrieval system, without written
permission from the Publisher, except in accordance with the
provisions of the Copyright Act, Act 98 of 1978.

Copy editing by Pat Tucker
Layout by Quba Design and Motion
Translation by Harry Kalmer
Proofreading by Elsabé Birkenmayer
This edition printed and bound by Creda

CONTENTS

Advocate Abram Fischer, KC (1908–1975).

WHO WAS BRAM FISCHER?

George Bizos SC

The Bram Fischer Waltz, a one-man play written by Harry Kalmer, is worthy of being read and staged more often.

It dramatises Bram's experience in a tiny prison cell. He relates his childhood on an Orange Free State farm, playing with the children of the black workers; the freedom and love bestowed in him by his father, mother and grandparents, who played an important role in the battle against the British occupation of the Boer republics; and his father's role as counsel to those who opposed the surrender and the involvement of the Union in the First World War.

He remembers his student days in South Africa and at Oxford University, his visit to the Soviet Union and the influence that Marxism had on him in relation to the treatment of black people in South Africa.

He pays homage to Molly, talks about his time at the Johannesburg Bar, the Communist Party, the happy family of Ruth, Ilse and Paul in the Beaumont Street house, which was open to many of us, irrespective of the colour of our skins.

He speaks to himself about what he remembers, particularly about the happiness he had with Molly and his dreams of the times when they danced, but also blames himself for the unfortunate event that led to her death. He mourns the unfortunate, lonely death of their son Paul.

In reading the play or seeing it we should bear in mind what is generally known about Bram Fischer.

At the first Bram Fischer Memorial Lecture organised by the Legal Resources Centre, President Nelson Mandela said:

With that background he could not but have become an Afrikaner nationalist, as we became African nationalists thirty years later as a result of our oppression by whites. Both of us changed. Both of us rejected the notion that our political rights were to be determined by the colour of our skins. We embraced each other as comrades, as brothers, to fight for freedom for all in South Africa, to put an end to racism and exploitation.

Bram was a senior counsel in the Rivonia Trial. He was arrested and charged, with others, with being a member of the Communist Party. Given permission to travel to the United Kingdom to argue a case, he came back but decided that he should go underground. He was arrested, charged with sabotage, a capital offence then, and was convicted. Sydney Kentridge and I advised that he should follow Nelson Mandela's example and make a statement from the dock. This is what he said:

I am on trial, My Lord, for my political beliefs and for the conduct which those beliefs drive me to. My Lord, when a man is on trial for his political beliefs and actions, two courses are open to him. He can either confess to his transgressions and plead for mercy, or he can justify his beliefs and explain why he has acted as he did. Were I to ask for forgiveness today, I would betray my cause. That course, My Lord is not open to me. I believe that what I did was right ...

My Lord, there is another reason, and a more compelling reason for my plea ... I accept, My Lord, the general rule that for the protection of a society laws should be obeyed. But when the laws themselves become immoral and require the citizen to take part in an organised system of oppression ... then I believe that a higher duty arises.

My conscience, My Lord, does not permit me to afford these laws such recognition as even a plea of guilty would involve. Hence, though I shall be convicted by this Court, I cannot plead guilty. I believe that the future may well say that I acted correctly.

In 1994 we asked for his reinstatement on the roll of advocates, even though he had died by then.

We approached Judge President Ngoepe of the Transvaal Provincial Division to appoint a full bench of three judges to hear an application on behalf of Bram's daughters, Ruth and Ilse. He readily responded that he would preside at such an application and that he would appoint two other judges to constitute a court, the composition of which would have pleased Bram. Ngoepe, an African, asked a white Afrikaner woman, Judge Snyders, who wrote the judgement for the court, and an Indian male, Judge Ponnan.

In her judgement Judge Snyders said:

The application of Bram Fischer's removal was heard by a full bench of this division. It was, in our view, therefore appropriate that the application for this reinstatement also [be heard] before a full bench; but even more appropriately, before a court as representative of the diversity of our society as possible. This is the kind of society that Fischer fought for. The future time to which reference is made in the judgement for his striking off has now arrived. The Society of Advocates recognises that Mr Fischer was a fit and proper person to continue to practise as an advocate. Mr Epstein, supported by Mr van der Linde on behalf of the General Council of the Bar of South Africa, submitted that a grave injustice was done to Abram Fischer. It fell to this court to rectify that injustice.

In the result and for the reasons stated, it took little urging from Mr Bizos, on behalf of the applicants, to persuade us to grant the order we made on 16 October 2003 for the reinstatement of Abram Fischer's name on the roll of advocates.

Some of his contemporaries may have considered him a failure. Even most of *them* now accept that he was *not*. He was one of the main pillars whose strength prevented a bloody revolution. He was a senior partner of Nelson Mandela in their efforts to avoid a bloody civil war. This is how he is and will continue to be remembered.

Only four of us went to his funeral in Bloemfontein – Chief Justice Rumpf saw us at the airport and asked what we were doing there when the Court was in recess. We said we had come to the Fischer funeral. Although an ardent supporter of the apartheid government, he said, 'Bram Fischer will be remembered long after many of us are forgotten.' The Chief Justice has been proved right.

LOOKING FOR BRAM FISCHER

Harry Kalmer

In 1985 Barney Simon, co-founder of the Market Theatre, saw a runthrough of my first play, *Bloed in die Strate* [*Blood in the Streets*] *(176 Interviews for Television)*.

Afterwards he commented that a script should serve as a springboard for a production, allowing the actors to leap. He felt that my staging of the play (a restaging of Jacqui Singer's 1984 production) did not do that.

It was a few days before opening night, and I suspect the entire production never got off the ground enough for the actors to reach the springboard.

To me, as a young playwright, working at the Market Theatre felt like being in the heart of South African theatre. In the Upstairs Theatre my white Anglo colleagues were doing Berkoff in British accents. Downstairs, our racially mixed play, combining two languages – 40% English, 60% Afrikaans – shared The Laager Theatre with the Zulu cast of Mbongemi Ngema's *Asinamali*.

It made me realise that South Africans, when we get to know each other, actually get along. One Friday we held the door so that the Berkoff cast could watch. On another night the entire Zulu-speaking cast of *Asinamali*, still dressed in their khaki prison uniforms, made up 90% of our audience.

Thirty years later I returned with *The Bram Fischer Waltz* to the venue where my friends had performed Berkoff. Barney Simon had died and the Upstairs Theatre had been renamed after him. Like the actors in *Asinamali*, David Butler, playing Bram Fischer, was dressed in prison khaki. At the back of my mind was Barney's advice: 'A script should only be a springboard for actors and directors.'

This is probably one of the reasons why this script contains so few stage directions – I would like each production to use it as its own springboard.

As a director I always try to stay out of the actors' way. Now that I am publishing my plays for the first time I realise this approach probably informs my theatre writing as well.

I was nine years old when Bram Fischer was arrested for the last time. I remember the photographs of Bram and his disguises in the newspapers. Shortly afterwards I read a book, *Rivonia: Masker Af!* [*Rivonia Unmasked*] by Lauritz Strydom (with forewords by Bram Fischer's nemeses, Percy Yutar, the prosecutor during the Rivonia Trial, and the then Minister of Justice, John Vorster) and realised that Bram Fischer was a dangerous man.

But growing up in the sixties also exposed me to hippies, to Paris 1968, to Woodstock and to the long-haired protestors disrupting the 1970 Springbok rugby tour. All these things were the antitheses of the dour white Afrikaners I encountered at school and church. That, combined with input from older siblings and my slightly more liberal English-speaking father, helped me realise by the age of 16 that Bram Fischer was probably one of the good guys.

I spent a year overseas in 1986/87. One of the things I did was to read books banned in apartheid South Africa: books like Steve Biko's *I Write what I Like* and Hugh Lewin's *Bandiet: Out of Jail*. One day I travelled to the International Defence and Aid Fund bookshop and bought *The Sun will Rise*, edited by Mary Benson and containing speeches from the dock by southern African political prisoners. I read the speech Bram had made during his trial and was moved to tears. I also came across Mary Benson's *Granta* article about Bram, 'A True Afrikaner'.

Back in South Africa I discussed with an actor friend the idea of doing a one-man play about Fischer. He mentioned the possibility to Barney, who chuckled and said he didn't have to read the article as he had been 'Mary's driver'. Only later did I realise that Barney wasn't being facetious. He and Mary Benson, one of the few people who supported Bram Fischer when he was underground, were close friends. Barney did probably drive her to some of their meeetings. A year earlier he had helped two of Nelson Mandela's Rivonia co-accused, Harold Wolpe and Arthur Goldreich, who had escaped from the cells at Marshall Square, leave the country.

In 2008 the 100th anniversary of Bram's birth passed almost unnoticed.

Shortly afterwards I read Steven Clingman's *Bram Fischer: Afrikaner Revolutionary* for the first time and started making notes. I realised I knew nothing about Fischer. I started gathering material, using, among other sources, Martin Meredith's *Fischer's Choice* and, much later, Hannes Haasbroek's *'n Seun soos Bram.*

For the second time I decided I wanted to write a play about Bram. I wanted to tell the story of a man who had contributed so much to the creation of a democratic South Africa but I also wanted to make a play that moved people the way only theatre can.

In 2011 I approached Adri Herbert, head of the Vryfees Arts Festival in Bloemfontein, for funding. I offered the part of Bram to David Butler because I knew he was interested in new South African work and is an accomplished solo performer in both English and Afrikaans. Later I also realised he looked a little like Bram. The play wasn't written yet, but David accepted the part. He was also interested in telling Fischer's story.

The Afrikaans version of the play opened in 2012 at the Vryfees in Bloemfontein and was also staged at several other Afrikaans arts festivals.

The English version was staged for the first time at the 2013 National Arts Festival and won the Standard Bank Silver Ovation Award. In 2014, at the same festival, it won the Adelaide Tambo award for celebrating human rights through the arts. It went on to play to capacity audiences at the Market Theatre and also returned to Bloemfontein in English.

The biographies of Clingman, Meredith and Haasbroek all provided vital information, but conversations with Bram's younger daughter, Ilse Wilson, and his fellow prisoners, Hugh Lewin and Denis Goldberg, offered different (often humorous) glimpses of the man. The importance of these brief conversations cannot be overemphasised. I learned things I otherwise would not have known. Bram was not only a committed activist but also a family man who loved throwing parties. He was a terrible dancer and enjoyed dop-en-dam (brandy and water).

After years of reading I wrote the play in less than six weeks. While it is historically accurate, it remains my interpretation of events. I wanted to write a play that both entertains and informs and to do that I chose to truncate, omit, simplify and alter.

I probably wrote the play because I wanted to understand Bram Fischer's reasons for making the choices he did. It was only when I translated his final speech from the dock, a document I had read for the first time almost 30 years before, that I found a possible answer.

Now I want readers and audiences to find their own answers.

TIMELINE/KEY MOMENTS

1908:	Abram ('Bram') Fischer is born in Bloemfontein on 23 April, the son of Percy and Ella Fischer
1925:	Matriculates from Grey College, Bloemfontein
1928:	Receives his BA degree from Grey University College (now the University of the Free State)
1928:	Represents the Orange Free State against the touring All Blacks in rugby
1929:	Serves as 'Prime Minister' of the South African Student Parliament
1931:	Completes his LLB at Grey University College
1932:	Arrives in Oxford, where he attends New College on a Rhodes Scholarship
1934:	Returns to South Africa after completing a law degree and diploma in Economics at Oxford
1935:	Admitted as an advocate (Johannesburg)
1937:	Marries Molly Krige
1939:	Birth of Ruth Fischer (daughter)
1942:	Elected to the Johannesburg Bar Council
1943:	Birth of Ilse Fischer (daughter)
1945:	Elected to Johannesburg District Committee of the Communist Party of South Africa
1945 (December):	Elected as member of the Central Committee of the Communist Party
1947:	Birth of Paul Fischer (son)
1948:	National Party comes to power in South Africa
1951:	Appointed King's Counsel
1956 (December):	Treason Trial begins
1960 (21 March):	Sharpeville Massacre
1961 (March):	Treason Trial concludes
1963 (11 July):	Raid on Liliesleaf Farm and the start of the Rivonia Trial
1964 (12 June):	Nelson Mandela and his co-accused, Ahmed Kathrada, Denis Goldberg, Govan Mbeki, Walter Sisulu, Andrew Mlangeni, Raymond Mhlaba and Elias Motsoaledi receive life sentences

1964 (13 June):	Death of Molly Fischer in a car accident
1964 (September):	Fischer is arrested
1964 (October):	Fischer arrives in London after being given permission to argue a case in the UK
1964 (November):	Fischer returns to South Africa
1965 (January):	Fischer goes underground
1965 (11 November):	Fischer is recaptured and tried under the Sabotage Act
1966 (6 May):	Fischer is given a life sentence
1967:	Awarded the Lenin Peace Prize
1971 (27 January):	Death of Paul Fischer
1975 (March):	Bram Fischer, still a prisoner, is released into his brother's care in Bloemfontein
1975:	Bram Fischer dies in Bloemfontein on 8 May
1985:	Denis Goldberg released from prison
1987:	Govan Mbeki released from prison
1989:	Ahmed Kathrada, Walter Sisulu, Andrew Mlangeni, Raymond Mhlaba and Elias Motsoaledi released from prison
1990 (2 February):	The African National Congress and Communist Party are unbanned
1990 (11 February):	Nelson Mandela is released from prison
1995:	President Nelson Mandela delivers the first Bram Fischer Memorial Lecture (organised by the Legal Resources Centre)
2003:	Bram Fischer becomes the first South African to be posthumously reinstated on the Roll of Advocates
2004:	Stellenbosch University awards Bram Fischer a posthumous honorary doctorate
2007:	Lord Joel Joffe delivers the first Bram Fischer Memorial Lecture at New College, University of Oxford
2012:	Bloemfontein International Airport is renamed Bram Fischer International Airport

The Afrikaans version of *The Bram Fischer Waltz* [*Die Bram Fischer Wals*] was first produced in 2012 at the Vryfees in Bloemfontein. The English version was staged for the first time at the 2013 National Arts Festival, Grahamstown.

The original production was directed by Harry Kalmer. Bram Fischer was played by David Butler and the voices were those of Amanda Strydom, Harry Kalmer and James Whyle.

'O Boereplaas' and 'The Red Flag', sung by Amanda Strydom, were interspersed throughout the play.

'Touch', by Hugh Lewin, © 2012 is quoted with permission from the author.

The Bram Fischer Waltz

Harry Kalmer

All the action takes place in a cell in the Pretoria Local Prison. The cell, 3.5 x 2.5 metres, stands in the middle of the stage. On the left [OP] is a poster of Bram as a baby, with his grandfather and father. On the right is a photograph of the actor playing Bram against the background of a red wall decorated with a hammer and sickle. In the cell there is a bed. [OP], a stool [centre stage] and a lectern.

The stage is a black box. The cell has walls made of bars 2.5 metres high. There are bars between the audience and the actor for the entire first scene. The bars fold open during the first blackout to make up the side walls and are folded back during the last blackout, once again forming a barrier between the audience and the actor. Costumes and props are all hidden under the bed.

SCENE 1

Lights up on **BRAM** *in the prison cell. He is dressed in khaki prison uniform.*

BRAM: These blessed candles of the night … [*Pause*]
Stars … Something else they took away from me …
Stars … can you believe it? That I would miss
something like that? When I was hiding on the farm
in the Magaliesberg I sometimes went walking in the
night to calm my thoughts. Just me and the sound of
my own breath. And my shadow … When there was
a moon. Sometimes I could hear the sounds of small
animals scurrying away in the bush … It made me feel
less alone. I wasn't used to loneliness yet … After all
these years I'm still not used to it. More often than not,
walking would calm my thoughts. And then I would
imagine that I was on commando 65 years before.
Alone in the veld with a bag of biltong and dried rusks.
Looking for British soldiers. [*He laughs and sings, to the
tune of* 'Sarie Marais']: 'Ek was so bang dat die Kakies
my sou vang en ver oor die see gaan wegstuur.'

Sometimes I felt so lonely that I would start talking
to the stars … O blessed candles of the night … Portia
in *Merchant of Venice*, if I remember correctly. If I was at
home I could have looked it up … Or asked Molly.

Molly Fischer, née Krige, whom I had to court
for seven years before she agreed to marry me …
Would I have fled if she was still alive? There was
water in the Sand River the night she drowned. The
same river where, 50 years before, the British signed
the convention that restored independence to the
Transvaal. Fifty years later they were back and this

time they colonised the Orange Free State as well. My mother was at the window when Lord Roberts and his army entered Bloemfontein. The khaki-clad soldiers looked like marching locusts.

The lances they used to spike the Boers like bush pigs at Elandslaagte and Paardeberg glistened in the sun. My mother fainted. That night her brother-in-law, Hugh Bidwell, removed the last Free State flag remaining in Bloemfontein; the one hanging in front of the Vierde Raadsaal …

On my 21st birthday he gave me a paperweight made of brass with a piece of that flag behind glass, as a gift. I kept it in my study at Beaumont Street until the very end. I wonder what happened to it? Probably gone. Like my rooms in Innes Chambers. Like the house in Beaumont Street. Like the cold white frost on the sports fields of Grey College on cold winter mornings. Like the hot summer afternoons on the farm. Like the brightly lit shop windows in Maitland Street in the Bloemfontein of my childhood. [*Pause*] Like my comrades in London … my comrades on Robben Island … Like my freedom … Like my Molly … Like my son Paul … Even like my daughters, Ruth and Ilse, waiting for me. So far, far away.

Like Job, I lost everything. But he was lucky. He could at least blame God. All I have to blame is Hendrik Frensch Verwoerd and John Vorster.

My Ouma Fichardt was a churchgoer. Presbyterian. But when the British invaded Bloemfontein the rest of the congregation turned their backs on her because she supported the Boers … As it is written in the 'Holy' Bible. Whited sepulchres … There are none so deaf as those who will not hear. Is that a metaphor or a verse from the Bible? Is there a difference?

My dear friend Leo Marquard once said that there was a lot of wisdom to be found in the Bible ... even if you didn't believe in it. Then he teased me and said that one could probably even be a better communist if you loved your neighbour like yourself [*Chuckles*]. And I was furious because he compared the science of Marxism to the superstition of religion. Mister Marquard, how I miss you now. Politically our ways parted a long time ago. But I learned so much from you. 'The devil can cite scripture for his purpose,' you quoted Shakespeare that afternoon to calm me down.

I have heard the devil citing scripture ... the Bible ... or even the even holier writ of a history written in the blood of the people. From dominees to Special Branch types ...

Even a book filled with love and history can be used to oppress.

I think there is a special place in hell for Gustav Preller and his Christian National histories. When you lie about history you lie about life. And the Nats will have to lie more and more. And the capitalists will allow them to do it. Because it is yet another way to justify the oppression of others: 'Just look what Dingane did to Piet Retief. One can't trust them.' And what the capitalists did to the Boer women and children is almost forgotten. Rendered harmless by the spire of the Women's Monument in Bloemfontein and the British pound ...

My Uncle Hugh and Emily Hobhouse were proof that it wasn't the English who wanted our diamonds, but the capitalists. And it wasn't the last time either – 1913, 1922, Sharpeville.

Distort history and call those who are different abusive names – 'hotnot', 'koelie' or 'kaffir' – but never call them a human being … It makes it easier to oppress them.

I was also raised like that. I even believed it. I remember the first time I shook a black man's hand in the Lawaaihoek location in Bloemfontein. I was 18 years old. I couldn't believe that I had shaken the hand of a black man.

I wandered through the streets of Bloemfontein all night. My head was spinning like a wooden top. When the sun rose I was at the edge of the location. The shacks gleamed in the morning light. A dog barked. A bucket filled with water. A baby started crying. A man lifted his hat and said: 'Môre baas.' I was 18 and he was grey. And for the first time in my life I understood how wrong it all was. I turned around and followed the old man. Back into town.

There were other people on that road. Black people. They all greeted me politely. The sun rose and shone on my arms. And it felt to me as if was walking a new road. And I wasn't alone. I'm still not alone.

Next to me is Hugh Lewin, the son of a missionary from Lydenburg; next to him Denis Goldberg, an engineer from Cape Town. Marius Schoon, the son of a Broederbond headmaster … then John Laredo, who loves N P van Wyk Louw so much. And so I can go on. Through the entire white political section of Pretoria Local. Through the entire country, from the Transvaal to the Cape. To Robben Island, where Nelson, Walter, Govan and all the others are waiting … Waiting for the day we will walk free. Free men in a free South Africa.

Last night I dreamed that Nelson was the state president, complete with Blackie Swart's high top hat and oranje-blanje-blou sash. Govan Mbeki was prime minister. And yours truly was the minister of justice in a large office in the Union Buildings, behind my large desk from Innes Chambers on top of a large government-issue carpet. There was a knock on the door. I opened the door. Molly was standing there. Our dead son, Paul, was behind her ... And then I realised that it was just a dream...

Fade to dark. We hear music: 'O Boereplaas'. While the music plays a spotlight shines on the photo of Bram, his father, Percy, and his grandfather, Abraham.

SCENE 2

The lights come up slowly.

BRAM: There is a photograph somewhere ... At least it was somewhere ... In my mother's house I think ... Who knows what happened to it ... But I remember it well ... My father is standing behind me with his huge moustache ... My grandfather next to him with his long beard ... I think I remember the day the photograph was taken ... But the date at the bottom reads 1910 ... So I could have been 18 months old at the most. Yet I swear I can remember that day. My father with his Edwardian moustache ... My oupa with his Boerebaard. Me in my little dress.

Do I really remember it or am I using the photograph as evidence? The way we lawyers do?

But I do remember three years later ... The roads surrounding Bloemfontein were filled with African people on donkey carts and shelters made from branches. The results of the 1913 Natives' Land Act ... 'Eleven years after the English trampled us into the ground we are helping them to do the same to the black man,' my father Percy said ... Once again how much of memory is imagination?

In 1932, while I was at Oxford, I visited the Soviet Union. The railway stations of the Ukraine were filled with peasants with small bundles of posssesions. The Intourist guides who accompanied us couldn't, or wouldn't, say where all these people were headed, but those peasants were as scared and confused as the black people in 1913 in Bloemfontein.

Yesterday in the prison garden I picked up a rock and

smelt it. I smelt the soil of Bergendal, the farm we had to move to when I was seven years old.

My father was also an advocate and decided in 1914 to defend some of the Afrikaner rebels who took up arms to protest against South Africa's participation in the Great War. As his colleagues had warned him, it turned out to be a mistake. He lost half his practice because he lost half his clients. He was even thrown out of the Bloemfontein Club. Just because he decided to defend those whose cause he supported. Against all odds.

To me, the farm was a whole lot of fun. My dad and I walked in the veld for hours. He taught me the names of the grasses, animals and even stones and identified things he saw. The droppings of an antelope. The hair ball of an owl. The pestilential purple Scottish thistle that travelled to South Africa in the fodder of the English soldiers' horses during the Boer War.

On the farm I had two small friends. We spent a lot of time in the veld. We made clay oxen, played kick the can and swam. I can't remember their names … I recall the smell of the soil, but not their names. Perhaps it was intentional. Because when we moved back to town, I was exactly the same as all the other white people. Black people were there to serve and nothing more. But on the farm the fact that I was white and they were black changed nothing in the way we played, laughed and fought with each other. We were friends. And that night in 1927 when I stayed awake because I had shaken a black man's hand I remembered my friends but not their names. Not even then. But to this day I remember how we used to play kleilat. The balls of clay we flung at each other left blue marks on my body. The marks on their bodies were black.

Letting the house in Reitz Street and moving to the farm with four children and a pregnant wife did not help my father earn enough to keep bread on the table. Mother started selling flowers at the station. Probably a tiny bit humiliating for the daughter of the Fichardts, one of the richest families in Bloemfontein, and the daughter-in-law of the former prime minister of the Orange River Colony.

But that was Mother for you. She supported my father. She even went to visit some of the rebels in jail. I remember the Kroonstad commandant who gave me a chameleon he had carved from wood to pass the time in prison.

My father was at Cambridge during the Boer War, while his brother was on commando, fighting the British. Perhaps that was his way of helping our people … these raw, naïve Boers who were prepared to take on the British imperialists and who were prepared to die for what they believed in. Just like Nelson and all the others.

My father must have known they didn't stand a chance. Yet he didn't hesitate to defend them. Mother supported him. Just like Molly supported me until she died.

Mother took me along when she took flowers and food to the rebels in prison. [*He laughs*]. It was my first taste of jail. Some of the Boers had already turned gray, but they were still proud and erect, with their beards reaching their chests as if they wanted to tell the world, 'Ek is 'n Boer [I am a Boer].' You could see that some of the people were lower class … Probably the sons of bywoners looking for adventure. My dad took on their

cases regardless … Because they needed his help …
Because no one else wanted to.

[*He wraps his arms around his body*] I wonder if the
rebels were this cold in their cells? I want to feel the sun
on my arms again. Be with my wife and children and
feel the beach sand between my toes. I want to kick a
rugby ball so that it flies through the air and lands in a
spray of dry yellow grass. In 1928 I played scrumhalf
for the Free State against the All Blacks. That was three
years before Danie Craven played his first test. I want
to dance with my wife, drink with my comrades and
swim in the swimming pool of the house in Beaumont
Street, embraced by the blue, with only air bubbles for
company.

BRAM *dives. We hear a splash. Light changes to an underwater
blue and we hear bubbles underwater.*

Ilse, my darling, I've written you a note – a little bit
formal – because it may fall into the hands of the police.
Even this may, but you can read it and tear it up if you
wish.

The sun is pouring into our garden and presently
I will wake you and we will go out for what will be
one of our last swims. We will look around at what
has become a lovely place and both our hearts will be
breaking because we will know that, inevitably, and
quite apart from my decision, explained in my other
letter, we will have to leave it all.

Ours has been a lovely home, with a beautiful
garden. Many, many years ago when old man Hutton
and I used to catch the bus together he said to me that
our garden would one day become a showpiece, and

that came true. But to me the garden and home have always been much more than a showpiece. They have been a sort of epitome of all that Molly was and what she stood for – friendliness and warmth, strength and love … [*He shouts*] God, what a terrible thing I did when I had that accident.

The lights change back to general. **BRAM** *recovers.*

Later that morning I crouched in the back of the Volkswagen so that Ilse could drop me off in Killarney. It was the start of my life underground. While I was on the run I would sometimes walk past the house late in the evening. There was no sign of the happiness my family and I had experienced there. I was on my own and on the run in Johannesburg, the place where people have learnt not to look too closely, because if they do they will see that the city wasn't built on gold, but on the sweat of cheap labour. I, too, was part of that stream of gold … Perhaps it was me who showed Sir Ernest Oppenheimer how not to pay a penny in taxes, but that money allowed me and Molly to do other work ... Important work … Unpaid work … To save my comrades from prison, from the gallows. What would have happened if they had executed Nelson, Walter, Denis, Kathy and all the others?

Everybody was convinced they were going to hang. Some thought that their deaths would ignite the revolution. But that was a dream.

The outside world would have been upset for a day or two. And then they would have forgotten. The Nats would have done anything to stay in power. Sharpeville … I rest my case, My Lord … And when the unrest following the executions had subsided we would still be stuck with Verwoerd and Vorster.

But if the people could have heard Nelson on the day that he was sentenced, there probably would have been a revolution. For five hours he read out his statement, in which he carefully explained why the ANC had decided to take up arms. And after five hours he put down his papers and looked the judge straight in the eye.

> 'During my lifetime I have dedicated myself to the struggle of the African people. I have fought against white domination and I have fought against black domination. I have cherished the ideal of a democratic and free society in which all persons live together in harmony and with equal opportunities. It is an ideal which I hope to live for and to achieve. But if needs be, My Lord, it is an ideal for which I am prepared to die.'

And then he was done. For a long time there was silence. In the gallery a woman sobbed. Even the judge looked moved. The weasel, Percy Yutar, the state prosecutor, fiddled with his papers. The judge said: 'You may call your next witness.' My next witness was Walter Sisulu.

Snap black out. Darkness. We hear cell doors closing and keys turning.

SCENE 3

Lights up on **BRAM**. *He takes a half loaf of bread from his shirt and places it on the floor; takes a piece of newspaper and a red pen from his underpants; rolls the paper into tubes and colours the tip of each 'candle' red. When five or six candles have been placed in the bread he holds it towards the audience and sings a birthday song usually sung to very small children.*

BRAM: Veels geluk liewe maatjie
   Omdat jy verjaar
   Mag die … [*hesitates before he replaces 'Here' with 'rooi vlag'*]
   Jou seën
   En nog baie jare spaar.

BRAM [*talking now*]: Liewe maatjie … Liewe Molly …
   Liewe Molly, you are the best maatjie I ever had.
   You made me the man I am. Without you I wouldn't have been where I am. I would probably never have led the life I did. I would have been sitting on the stoep of the Johannesburg Country Club drinking gin and tonic along with all the other scared whites. But with you at my side that was never an option.
   Dear Molly, at six the cell doors open. We report for roll call. After roll call it is breakfast – mieliepap and lekker volgraanbrood baked by our fellow prisoners; 'coffee' – 75% burnt mielies and chicory and 6% coffee. Then we sew post bags or work in the garden.
   The post bags break my heart. You know how much

I love writing letters. I prefer gardening. The smells remind me of Beaumont Street and the farm. At noon they serve us samp, potatoes and a weak excuse for a piece of meat and, after Jock Strachan gave that information to the *Rand Daily Mail* about the conditions of political prisoners, peanut butter three times a day. At 4 pm they lock us up … first the gate, then the door. I am on my own for 14 hours.

The lights start dimming. We hear a male voice whispering: Bram!

BRAM: 6 am doors open … roll call. After roll call, mieliepap … volgraan bread baked by our fellow prisoners; 'coffee', 75% mielies, 6% coffee grounds. Post bags, gardening. The post bags break my heart. You know how much I like writing letters. Gardening is better.

We hear a male voice – a more insistent whisper: Bram!

BRAM: The smells remind me of Beaumont Street. At 12 noon potatoes and an excuse for meat … Strachan … peanut butter … three times … At four they lock us up. Gate and then the door, 14 hours I am on my own.

MALE VOICE: Bram!

The delivery gets more intense.

BRAM: 6 am the door opens … roll call … pap bread … burnt chicory … post bags … Beaumont Street …

The lights start to fade.

MALE VOICE: Bram!

BRAM: … mielies and meat … bags, work … soup … peanut butter … gate door … 14 hours …

The delivery gets more intense. The stage is dark now.

MALE VOICE [*shouting*]: Bram!

BRAM: 6 am the doors open … fall in … porridge … burnt … post bags fingers … Beaumont Street … meat … work … soup … gate door … hours … gate door dark hours 14 dark hours.

MALE VOICE: Bram!

BRAM [*finally reacting*]: Denis, is that you?

Silence.

BRAM: Hugh, is that you?

Silence.

BRAM: Marius, is dit jy?

Silence.

BRAM: John, is dit jy?

Silence.

BRAM [*panicky*]: Denis … [*waits for reaction*]. Hugh …
[*waits*]. Marius … [*waits*]. John …

BRAM [*panic growing*]: Denis … Hugh … Marius … John
… Denis? Hugh? Marius? John? Antwoord my …
Denis, Hugh, Marius, John.

WOMAN'S VOICE: Bram!

BRAM [*calms down*]: Molly?

WOMAN'S VOICE: Sshhh.

BRAM: Ma Ella?

WOMAN'S VOICE [*louder*]: Sshhh!

BRAM: Ouma?

WOMAN'S VOICE [*louder still*]: Sshhh!

BRAM: Tannie Tibbie?

WOMAN'S VOICE: Sshhh!

BRAM: Molly?

WOMAN'S VOICE: Sshhh!

BRAM: Ruth?

WOMAN'S VOICE: Sshhh!

BRAM: Ilse?

WOMAN'S VOICE: Sshhh. Don't worry.

BRAM: Who are you?

WOMAN'S VOICE: Don't worry, Bram … The night shall soon pass. The sun will rise again … Die son sal weer opkom … de zon sal weer rijzen.

SCENE 4

Spotlight on **BRAM** *at lectern in advocate's robes. He refers to his notes throughout.*

BRAM: Met vertrouwen leggen wij onze zaak open voor de gehele wereld. Het zij wij overwinnen, het zij wij sterven: de vrijheid zal in Afrika rijzen als de zon uit de morgenwolken.

I am on trial, My Lord, for my political beliefs and for the conduct which those beliefs drove me to. My Lord, whatever labels may have been attached to the 15 charges brought against me, they all arise from me having been a member of the Communist Party and from my activities as a member of that party. I engaged upon those activities because I believed that in the dangerous circumstances which have been created in South Africa it was my duty to do so.

My Lord, when a man is on trial for his political beliefs and actions, two courses are open to him. He can either confess his transgressions and plead for mercy or he can justify his beliefs and explain why he acted as he did.

Lights dip and up to indicate time lapse.

The laws under which I am being 'persecuted' were enacted by a wholly unrepresentative body, a body in which three-quarters of the people of this country have no voice whatsoever. These laws were enacted not to prevent the spread of communisim but to silence the voices of the large majority of our citizens from being heard by a government intent on depriving

31

them, solely on account of their colour, of the most elementary human rights.

Lights dip and up to indicate time lapse.

My first duty, then, is to explain to the court that South Africa's problems can only be satisfactorily solved by the application of that scientific system of political knowledge known as Marxism. [*Aside*] I didn't use the word blood bath or war, but it was implied.

I have to cast my mind back more than a quarter of a century in order to precisely ascertain what my motives were for joining the Communist Party.

In my mind there remain two clear reasons for my approach to the Communist Party. The one is the glaring injustice which exists in our country, the other is a gradual realisation, as I became more and more involved with the Congress Movement, that it was always the members of the Communist Party who were prepared to sacrifice the most, to give of their best in the struggle against discrimination and poverty.

Lights dip and up to indicate time lapse.

BRAM [*addressing judge*]: I believe South Africa is heading for a civil war and that such a war will never be won by the whites … But win or lose, My Lord, the results will be shattering and lasting for this country. There is another obligation resting on my shoulders, My Lord. My actions mean that at least one Afrikaner is protesting actively. I am deeply concerned about a future where the Afrikaner will be blamed for all the evils and humiliation caused by apartheid. All this bodes ill for our future. It has bred amongst all non-whites a deep-rooted hatred for Afrikaners, for our language and our political and racial outlook.

To remove this barrier will demand all the wisdom, leadership and influence of Nelson Mandela and all those leaders now interned and imprisoned for their political beliefs. It demands also that Afrikaners themselves should protest openly and clearly against discrimination. Surely in such circumstances there is an additional duty laid on me: that at least one Afrikaner should make this protest actively and positively, even though as a result I now face 15 charges instead of four.

If, one day, my actions may help to establish a bridge across which white leaders and the real leaders of the non-whites can meet to settle the destinies of all of us by negotiating and not by force of arms I shall be able to bear with fortitude any sentence which this court may impose on me.

Lights dip and up to indicate time lapse.

I concluded with Paul Kruger's words about the struggle of the Boers against the British in 1881. 'Met vertrouwen leggen wij onze zaak open voor de geheelde wereld. Het zij wij overwinnen, het zij wij sterven: de vrijheid zal in Afrika rijzen als de zon uit de morgenwolken [With confidence we place our case before the entire world. Whether we are victorious or whether we die, freedom will arise in Africa like the sun from the morning clouds.]'

Addresses audience.

And then I sat down on my own on the long bench that had been specially built for Nelson, Denis, Kathy, Walter, Raymond and all the others when I defended them in the Rivonia Trial in 1964. My last appearance in court was not as an advocate but as the accused.

I was sentenced to life imprisonment on 9 May 1966. I didn't wear my advocate's robe but a shirt Ilse, Ruth and Paul had bought me for my birthday. After I was sentenced I turned to them and gave the ANC salute ... Three konstabels led me from court. My advocate, George Bizos, stood looking at me from the advocate's bench. My life as bandiet 333166 had begun.

That night I dreamed about Molly.

Lights turn red. Bram turns his black robe inside out. It is lined in red. We hear a waltz. He dances, counting '1, 2, 3'.

I dreamed that we were dancing in our lounge in Beaumont Street. The floor was covered in chalk. Molly was wearing a red dress. Our children were sitting in a row against the wall drinking red cooldrink. There was a marquee outside in the garden. There were other guests ... comrades ... Nelson and Winnie ... Joe and Ruth ... Rusty and Hilda ... Walter and Albertina ... We danced and we laughed. And we were happy ....

Music stops. Lights go to general.

I woke up. And it was May and I was in Pretoria and it was freezing. It was May in Pretoria and I was in Pretoria Local. It was May in Pretoria and there were no panes in the window. It was as cold as a winter's night on the vlaktes of the Free State. 'Hoe koud is die windjie en skraal [How cold and chilly this wind is].'[1] The afterglow of the dream lingered for a while and I recalled how Molly told the children how I always counted out loud when we waltzed … [*He starts waltzing*] 1, 2, 3 step 1, 2, 3 step 1, 2, 3 step … The children didn't say anything. They knew their mother's musical ear was suspect. And I had a good reason for counting out loud. The first time I asked her for a waltz, in the Ramblers Club in Bloemfontein, she trampled my toes to pieces.

Music fades out.

But oh, she could make me happy. As happy as I was when I played the piano for the children. As happy as when I received a letter from my mother. Or when the sun shone on my arms. With her in my arms the world felt round again and things made more sense … Even if I had to count out loud to stop her from stepping on my toes.

Lights fade.

---

1. A line from one of the first major Afrikaans poems, 'Winternag', by Eugene Marais.

SCENE 5

BRAM [*facing the audience, puts shaving foam on his face
and starts shaving*]: The other night I dreamed I had a
long beard. A beard like Oupa Abraham. A beard like
old President Steyn of the Orange Free State. Like the
Commandant of the Kroonstad Kommando who gave
me the chameleon carved out of wood. As if he knew
that one day I would become a chameleon, pretending
to be Douglas Black, professional photographer …
When I told my dream to Marius Schoon he said: 'Oom
Bram, is Oom seker Oom het nie gedroom Oom is Karl
Marx nie? [Uncle Bram are you sure you didn't dream
that you were Karl Marx?]'

I laughed, and recalled my last visit to London. I
hopped on one of those red buses to clear my mind. To
escape everybody who was begging me not to return to
South Africa. I realised I was near Highgate Cemetery.
I got out … The previous time I went there I was
with Molly … It was easy to find Karl Marx's grave. I
stood looking at his big bearded head and the words
'Workers of all lands unite' and realised once again that
it wasn't only Marx's theories that had led me to the
Communist Party but also the need to serve my fellow
man.

I was arrested for the last time on 23 September 1964
under the Suppression of Communism Act. My trial
was scheduled for November. I applied for bail and,
contrary to all expectations, it was granted. I was even
allowed to travel to London to defend a case in front
of the Privy Council. I won the case. My comrades in
London, Joe Slovo and Yusuf Dadoo, even Ruth and
her husband, Anthony, tried to convince me to stay.

When Anthony said that a conviction would mean the end of my career I said, 'Fuck my career.' They were both shocked. But I had to come back. I gave them my word. Besides, the Nat government would have preferred it if I had fled the country.

There were enough comrades abroad to state our case overseas. I had to get back and organise the party internally. Even though I knew that the government was determined to jail me. Sagmoedige vriendelike, ordentlike Bram se moer [Fuck the decent, soft-spoken Bram]! Bram Fischer was ready to fight. On 2 November I was back in South Africa. On the 16th I was back in court. In the dock, not the advocate's bench. The first witness was my old friend Piet Beyleveld.

SCENE 6

Lights up on **BRAM** *with hat, tweed jacket, picnic basket and binoculars. He is short of breath. An African marching band slightly off-key, plays in the distance.*

BRAM [*calling to Molly and children offstage*]: Molly … Over here … Mens kan beter sien [One can see better] … Come Ruth … Ilse …

BRAM *takes out a handkerchief and wipes his face.*

Sjoe, it's a stiff climb up this hill isn't it … [*looks through binoculars*]. Just see how neat the stage is. And the people! The police tried to stop them from coming but it was in vain … Just look at all the people. How many people do you think there are, Molly? Look at the stalls … the ANC flags … the posters. Look girls: 'Equal rights for all.' It's like a church bazaar. You're not looking at a soccer field in Kliptown, kids … But at history being made. Look there's Oom Piet ... Uncle Piet Beyleveld…

The Special Branch and Blackie Swart's banning order prevent us from being there, Molly. But Piet Beyleveld is on the stage to keep the name of the communists high.

In the background we hear a voice reciting the Freedom Charter. BRAM mimes the activities of pouring tea, etc. Every now and then he lifts the binoculars. Claps and cheers.

Some people in the ANC said the communists hi-jacked the Freedom Charter. But it is not true. Rusty Bernstein may have written it, but his words were just the wishes of the grannies and mine workers written on brown OK Bazaars shopping bags. Thousands of little pieces of paper that were all over their house for months while they were working on it. The Freedom Charter wasn't written by the communists but by the wishes of the people of South Africa.

BRAM addresses the audience and changes back into prison gear.

At 3.30 on the afternoon of the second day the police struck … They said that those who were there were suspected of high treason. When the people realised what was going on, they started singing 'Nkosi Sikelel' iAfrika'.

We hear 'Nkosi Sikelel' iAfrika'.

The police interrogated everybody and confiscated everything. Even posters with the words 'Soup with meat' and 'Soup without meat'. They questioned people deep into the night. Nelson Mandela was also there but he escaped, dressed as a milkman.

Piet Beyleveld always had a way with words. During the war he was head of the broadcasting service for Afrikaans soldiers in Cairo … An anti-fascist to the bone and when he returned from the north he joined Sailor Malan's Torch Commando. Then he joined the trade unions and eventually ended up with me on the central committee of the South African Communist Party. By that time the party was totally underground.

Piet … Piet … was … so Afrikaans … If Piet is a

communist, I sometimes thought … Then I'm not betraying my own people. I am against the capitalists and the racists. Not my own people. It was good to hear Piet Beyleveld speak that day at the People's Congress …

But Piet was also not short of words when he was led into court on 16 November 1964 to act as state witness against me and the 13 other accused. He didn't look at me. But he also didn't look away. His voice was steady. Some of the others, like Jean Middleton and Eli Weinberg, looked at him in disgust. Piet didn't respond. After 90-days' solitary confinement his eyes were empty. Not the unfocused 1000-yard stare of a returning soldier. No! They were just … empty.

Piet's testimony convinced me even more that it was time to go underground. The South African Communist Party was destroyed, the ANC seriously wounded. Nelson, Walter, Govan, Kathy and all the others were on the island. It was time to go underground and reorganise … In 1962 they called Nelson the Black Pimpernel. It was time for a Boer Pimpernel. When the case resumed on Monday morning 25 January I wasn't in court. My advocate, Harold Hanson, read a letter to the court in which I explained the reason for my disappearance.

Lights go down.

SCENE 7

BRAM *sits on the bed, dejected.*

BRAM: Hugh Lewin, in the cell next to me, showed me a
poem he wrote. I read it a few times. It keeps turning
over and over in my mind:

I don't want fists and paws
I want
To want to be touched again
And to touch
I want to feel alive
Again
I want to say
When I get out
Here I am
Please touch me
Over and over I hear those words
Here I am
Please touch me

Hugh's sentence is almost over. He can start dreaming
about touch again. He only has a few months left.
Everyone is going to leave before me. Already I have
seen them come and go, the white politicals of Pretoria
Local. Issy Heyman, who was sentenced to five
years because he refused to testify against me. Hugh,
Marius, John Laredo, Baruch Hirson, Jack Tarshish, Eli
Weinberg and all the others are going to walk out free
men. Perhaps there will be a reunion one day of all the
white politicals of Pretoria Local. And Marius and John
Laredo and I will speak Afrikaans … And John will tell
us about a new Afrikaans book or poem that he has
read. And Denis will make a joke, as always.

The only thing is ... Denis and I have been sentenced to life imprisonment. Who knows when we will get out? Who knows when we will be touched again?

Shortly after his sentence, Denis said to his wife that he would understand if she wanted to leave him for another ... She was still young and who knew when he was going to walk free again ... I wonder if I would be able to do the same if Molly was still there?

But Molly wasn't there ... There was a cow ... There was a man on a motor cycle ... There was me, who jerked the steering wheel. There was the sound of the Mercedes bursting through the wire fence and donnering down the steep embankment. There was the quiet when we stopped on the banks of the Sand River. There were Liz Lewin and me clambering through the front windows. There was an unconscious Molly on the back seat. There was the struggle to try and get her out. There was the splash as the car tumbled into the river. The bubbles breaking the surface as it sank the 30 feet to the bottom of the river. There was me diving in vain. Time after time after time. My arme, arme vrou ... My arme vrou, my arme vrou [my poor wife] ... Never again will I smell the smell of her hair, hear her laughter or watch proudly as she makes a political point ... Never again will we dance in the lounge of the house in Beaumont Street.

We hear waltz music.

BRAM [*counting*]: 1, 2, 3 ...

Piet Beyleveld cracked after 90 days. I lasted for 290 days.

Lights fade.

SCENE 8

We hear the James Bond theme tune. **BRAM** *mimes the title sequence of the 1960s Bond movies.*

BRAM: The petit bourgeois press tried to make me look like a Boere James Bond … An Afrikaner terrorist and, of course, a traitor to my people.

   When it became obvious which way my trial was headed I decided to go underground. The morning Ilse dropped me in Killarney I was taken to Rustenburg in a Combi belonging to the Performing Arts Council of the Transvaal. I started playing my new role in a cottage in the Magaliesberg. The only people I saw were the old lady who lived in the main house on the farm and the man who drove me there … Raymond Schoop, a theatre designer who had survived the Nazis.

   Twice a week he would drive the 40 miles from Pretoria to coach me. He said I should not only hide but also create a whole new appearance and personality … He put me on a strict diet and showed me how to shave my hairline so that I could have a higher forehead, and how to dye my hair … He taught me to walk in a way that would hide my slight limp … He also made me smoke a pipe so that my voice would change.

   During my weeks on the farm I heard for the first time that the Johannesburg Bar was going to try and have me disbarred. I was furious. As an advocate I had always acted ethically, morally and fairly. My decision to go underground was political. During the rebellion of 1914 no steps were taken against people like my father who defended the rebels. Our Minister of Justice, Balthazar John Vorster, wasn't punished, even though he was interned in Koffiefontein as a Nazi supporter during the Second World War.

Raymond Schoop's disguise worked. When Ralph Sepel met me in the parking lot of the Marymount Maternity Home he didn't recognise me at first. Even Ilse thought I was somebody else. One morning in Commissioner Street a security policeman who had followed me several times in the past, and even interrogated me once, looked me in the face without recognising me. I got into a lift with my friend Pat Davidson and started talking to her … She didn't recognise me.

But alas, my attempts to contact new comrades and rebuild structures were less successful. I wrote a few letters to the newspapers … and to Beyers Naudé, in the hope of getting white South Africans to enter a debate. The money from London didn't arrive as regularly as it was supposed to and the couple they were going to send to support me never arrived. By the time the false passport finally got here, my dreams of leaving the country every few weeks to address meetings in London and New York and then return incognito had all but disappeared. By then, loneliness was my greatest enemy. And my main aim was to stay out of the hands of the Special Branch.

Pat Davidson, Ilse, Violet Weinberg, Lesley Schermbrucker, Mary Benson and Ralph Sepel and his wife supported me.

Pat took me to the Kruger Park Game Reserve. The day that my fellow accused in the trial were sentenced Mary Benson and I had a picnic in Volksrust.

'If you were there today they would have sentenced you to only five years,' said Mary.

I got angry and shouted that she was like all the other petite bourgeoisie who wanted me to go to court and say that I did what I did because I was a humanist rather than a communist. I am a Marxist. I will not apologise to anybody.

Mary looked at me with a raised eyebrow and said: 'petite bourgeoisie?' She folded the picnic rug and started packing the leftovers into the picnic basket.

We hardly spoke on the way back to Johannesburg. We stopped in Heidelberg to buy hair dye. She dropped me outside the house in Waverley where I was hiding and said: 'You know, Bram, I will never understand how a man as intelligent as you can be a communist.'

I turned away angrily and walked back to the house, forgetting to hide my limp.

That night the Oude Meester and I fell into deep conversation. I listened to a record of Brecht poems set to the music of Eisler.

We hear 'Das Lied von der Moldau'.

I listened over and over to 'Das Lied von der Moldau' … 'The great won't stay great, the order is turning, the night has twelve hours then comes the dawn.' Every time the song was over I would get up and start playing it again.

'Das ist sehr schön' … A voice spoke behind me … I froze and slowly turned round … At first I thought the man in the door was Special Branch. Then I noticed the two fountain pens in his shirt pocket. He was a short man with a dark beard, a hat and a pair of D F Malan spectacles. My German left me.

'Yes it is,' I replied.

'This is the music of my youth,' the man said in

English. 'I was in Berlin during those years. Brecht, Weill, Eisler … I just got away in time. Arrived in 1937 on the *SS Stuttgart* in Cape Town. Pirow and his grey shirts were on the quay. In Stellenbosch Verwoerd was complaining because the government allowed too many Jews into the country. I felt out of place. But what could I do? I wasn't welcome in Germany anymore. People told me there were more Jews and fewer Afrikaners in Johannesburg. It is true … I am happy here.

I nodded my head and offered him a drink. He accepted. But somebody had drunk all the Oude Meester while I wasn't watching. The man smiled politely and said that it was alright. Then he asked if he could listen to the 'Das Lied von der Moldau' again. I played the song again. He sat down and hummed under his breath. When the song was done he got up.

'Why are communists such good poets?' he asked.

I wondered if the man recognised me.

'Brecht, Neruda, Éluard, Hikmet', he continued. 'Brilliant poets … all of them.'

I smiled politely and nodded.

'Perhaps it is because they are such good dreamers,' he smiled and walked out of the door.

It was the second time that day somebody had called me a dreamer.

I realised that in future I would have to keep the front door locked.

After the stranger left I missed Molly. I looked for a waltz record that would remind me of her. The music was not really what we normally danced to but it was all I had. I danced all over the lounge, pretending that she was in my arms.

A few months later, 290 days after going underground, I was arrested.

My advocate, George Bizos, asked me whether sacrificing my family's happiness and my career was worth it. I asked him if he had asked Nelson Mandela the same question.

I still hear the music from that night in Waverley. When things get too much …

We hear waltz music. **BRAM** *starts waltzing.*

I imagine myself dancing with Molly. On important days like the anniversaries of her death and Paul's and on Ruth's and Ilse's birthdays I make a point of getting up from the bed to dance. But mostly I just lie on the bed and imagine myself performing the dance steps while I count out loud. Sometimes I dream Molly and I are dancing. And that we dance from my cell into the courtyard of Pretoria Local Prison and then we waltz faster and faster until we take off and the street lights and the jacaranda trees grow small and we spin and turn and dance … And dance … until we land in the lounge of our house in Beaumont Street.

BRAM *dances faster and faster until the lights go dark.*

SCENE 9

Lights come up red. We hear a woman's voice. **BRAM** *is covered with a red communist flag, with yellow hammer and sickle.*

FVO: Bram Fischer never danced out of the gates of
Pretoria Local. By the time he left the prison, on
25 March 1975, he was 66 years old and dying of
cancer. His last months in prison were a hell of pain,
suffering, bureaucratic brutality, official indifference
and the petty politics of the Minister of Justice, Jimmy
Kruger, who refused to release him into the care of his
daughters in Johannesburg.

Bram was taken to Bloemfontein. His brother Paul's
home was declared a prison. Visitors, and even mail,
were subject to prison regulations. Fischer was still
a prisoner. Sometimes he would sit on the verandah
with his daughter, his granddaughter and other family
members. Mostly he was bedridden. On 8 May 1975,
after two weeks in a coma. Bram Fischer passed away.

His funeral was small and attended only by his
family and a few friends. The authorities confiscated
his ashes immediately. More than a year later, without
the knowledge of his family, his remains were strewn
in an unknown place in Bloemfontein.

Darkness. We hear 'Das Lied von der Moldau' as the audience leaves the auditorium.

Alternative closing scene:

The bars are back between the audience and the actor. **BRAM** *addresses the audience.*

BRAM: I never danced out of the gates of Pretoria Local. By the time I left the prison, on 25 March 1975, I was 65 years old and dying of cancer. My last months in prison were a hell of pain, suffering, bureaucratic brutality, official indifference and the petty politics of the Minister of Justice, Jimmy Kruger, who refused to release me into the care of Ilse and Ruth in Johannesburg. I was taken to Bloemfontein. My brother Paul's home was declared a prison. Visitors, and even mail, were subject to prison regulations. I was still a prisoner. Sometimes I would sit on the verandah with my daughters, my granddaughter and other family members. But most of the time I was bedridden. On 8 May 1975, after two weeks in a coma, I died.

My funeral was small and attended by my family and a few friends. The authorities confiscated my ashes immediately. More than a year later, without telling my family, they scattered my remains in an unknown place in Bloemfontein.

Darkness. We hear 'Das Lied von der Moldau' as the audience leaves the auditorium.

BRAM FISCHER – THE POWER OF MORAL COURAGE

Yvonne Malan

It does not matter how many people chose moral duty over the rationality of self-preservation – what does matter is that some did. Evil is not all-powerful. It can be resisted. The testimony of the few who did resist shatters the authority of the logic of self-preservation. It shows it for what it is in the end – a choice.

Zygmunt Bauman[1]

Introduction

President Nelson Mandela was beloved by all race groups in South Africa. His life and legacy have been honoured around the globe with a Nobel Peace Prize, countless honorary degrees, documentaries and books. He was mourned by the entire world on an unprecedented scale never likely to be repeated. But far fewer people know the name of the man who saved Mandela from the gallows during the Rivonia Trial. That man was Bram Fischer.

Fischer died nearly 20 years before South Africa's transition to democracy, but that is not the only reason why he is largely unknown: the apartheid government intended him to be forgotten. After his death in 1975 the government did its best to erase Fischer from the landscape. His ashes were confiscated (they were never recovered). His words and image were banned. In pre-1994 history books Fischer appeared – if he appeared at all – as a ghostly silhouette, his face whited out to appease the apartheid censors.

The Bram Fischer Waltz introduces Fischer's story to a new audience. Harry Kalmer's play encapsulates many of the key moments in Fischer's life, from his boyhood days in the Free State to his eventual imprisonment for his political activities. But Kalmer achieves more than merely relaying biographical details. He portrays Fischer as much more than the Rivonia defence counsel or 'volksverraaier' (traitor to his people). Bram Fischer was also a son, a husband, a father, a loyal comrade. And, just as importantly, he was the embodiment of moral courage.

The play ends in 1975 with Fischer's death from cancer. His friends and comrades would still spend more than a decade on Robben Island and in Pretoria Central Prison.

Fischer died during the darkest days of apartheid. The man who many thought might one day become prime minister died a prisoner. 'His' people, the Afrikaners, viewed him as a communist traitor, a man who tragically 'threw away' his life for a lost cause.

Bram Fischer did sacrifice and suffer for his cause. But he never regretted his decision to oppose apartheid, even if it meant a life sentence. After the conclusion of the Rivonia Trial he was aware that his days as a free person were numbered. He could have remained in the United Kingdom in 1964, where he was arguing a case before the Privy Council, but he returned to South Africa, knowing what his fate would be. He never wavered in his belief that apartheid would end. He certainly did not view his decisions and their consequences as tragic. And he did not die for a 'lost cause'. His vision of a non-racial democracy triumphed; his legacy of moral courage and non-racialism endured long after his death.

Bram Fischer's story deserves to be remembered and honoured, not merely because of his historical role, but also because his life raises fundamental questions about the theory and practice of moral courage, non-racialism and the complexity of identity.

Biography

Abram (Bram) Fischer was born in Bloemfontein on 23 April 1908 into a prominent Afrikaner family. He was the first child of Percy and Ella Fischer – three brothers, Paul, Gustav and Piet, and a sister, Ada, would follow. His grandfather, Abraham, was the last prime minister of the Republic of the Orange Free State. His father, Percy, graduated from Cambridge University, served as a judge of the Free State Supreme Court, and later became judge president of the Orange Free State Province. His family members were proud Afrikaners and Nationalists.

Abraham Fischer served in President M T Steyn's Cabinet during the Anglo-Boer War. Percy Fischer supported the 1914 Rebellion, despite the cost to his professional career. Much was expected of Bram. He attended Grey College, where he played for the first rugby and cricket teams and he was junior tennis champion of the Free State. He matriculated in 1925 with a first-class pass. After a year at the University of Cape Town he transferred to Grey University College (now the University of the Free State), partly to give himself a better chance of winning a prestigious Rhodes scholarship. He received both his BA and his LLB from this university.

He also became involved in student politics and was elected Nationalist 'Prime Minister' of the South African student parliament in 1929. Many people believed – and with good reason – that this was merely an audition for the real position.

He was intelligent, talented and charismatic and any number of prominent positions – from judge to prime minister – beckoned. When he turned 21 Mrs Steyn, widow of the former president of the Free State Republic, wrote: 'I know that Bram Fischer is going to play an honourable role in the history of South Africa.' As Fischer's biographer,

Stephen Clingman, notes, 'It was a prophecy that was destined to be true, but not in a way that Mrs Steyn or anyone else ... would have foreseen.'[2]

Three years later Fischer was awarded a Rhodes scholarship. He arrived in Oxford in January 1932 and quickly settled into life at New College, whose motto, 'Manners Makyth Man', encapsulates much of his extraordinary life.

A popular member of the Rhodes and New College communities, Fischer obtained a degree in law, followed by a diploma in economics. He represented New College in tennis and rugby, a serious knee injury preventing him from possibly achieving a 'Blue'. He attended black-tie dinners at Rhodes House and was a member of the famed Oxford Union. Along with a few close friends he travelled through Europe, seeing both the rise of fascism and the new communist Russia at first hand. Many would later speculate that this was when Fischer became a communist, although the exact date has never been established.

Fischer corresponded regularly with his family, writing to his father in Afrikaans and to his mother in English, often discussing politics, both European and South African. He was also a young man in love, corresponding frequently with Molly Krige, whom he had met in 1930.

At the end of 1934 he returned to South Africa to begin his legal career. The following year he was admitted as an advocate (Transvaal Division of the Supreme Court of South Africa). Although he became best known for his involvement in political trials, those only came later in his career. In his early years at the Bar he was involved in a variety of cases, from libel to criminal.

As his career progressed he represented mining houses and became an expert on water rights. Despite his 'radical' politics, he was a well-liked and respected member of the Bar. He was first elected to the Johannesburg Bar Council in 1942 and served, with the exception of three years, until 1963, including a term as president from 1960 until 1961. When he was appointed King's Counsel (the equivalent of the current Senior Counsel) in 1951, he was personally congratulated by the Minister of Justice, C R 'Blackie' Swart, who knew Fischer and his Free State family. Swart was to play a fundamental role in the introduction of the Suppression of Communism Act, a piece of legislation that would have significant consequences for Bram Fischer.

In 1945 Fischer was elected a member of the Johannesburg district committee of the Communist Party and, later, to its Central Committee. Raised in a Nationalist household, he had little sympathy for British imperialism and would eventually come to see his communism and his commitment to non-racialism as natural successors to his anti-imperialist sentiments. However, he was never anti-English, was never a fanatical Nationalist and, unlike many of his Afrikaner peers, never joined the Afrikaner Broederbond, the secret organisation of white Afrikaner men which played a key role in shaping apartheid policies. He was proud of his Afrikaner heritage but his commitment to justice allowed him to transcend the limits of a narrow understanding of identity, a quality partly resulting from the fact that his family was more cosmopolitan than many of their Afrikaner contemporaries and partly from the influence of another key figure in his political development, Leo Marquard, a teacher at Grey College, who challenged his pupils to think for themselves.

When Fischer was a student Marquard involved him in projects which allowed him, for the first time to meet black South Africans as equals rather than as servants. These meetings had a profound effect on him, as he later noted in his statement from the dock. At Oxford he was exposed to a much wider world and to rigorous debate. Whatever the date may have been of his officially joining the Party, his commitment to the equality of all human beings preceded it.

Family always played a central role in Bram Fischer's life, as *The Bram Fischer Waltz* makes clear. Fischer married Molly Krige in 1937 and the couple settled in Johannesburg. Two years later their first child, Ruth, was born. Another daughter, Ilse, was born a few years later, followed by a son, Paul, who was diagnosed with cystic fibrosis and was not expected to live more than six years. His parents made every effort to make his life as normal as possible and, despite the odds, he lived long enough to graduate from university.

Molly Fischer, too, was a political activist. She organised collections for the Communist Party, helped in various campaigns and stood as a candidate in the Johannesburg City Council election in 1945. Nelson Mandela described her as 'a wonderful woman, generous and unselfish, utterly without prejudice. She had supported Bram in more ways than it was possible to know. She had been a wife, colleague and a comrade.'[3] She, too, would pay a price for her political convictions. She was arrested, detained, and served with banning orders as the National Party, which had come to power in 1948, became increasingly rigorous in its oppression of opponents.

The Suppression of Communism Act, which came into force in 1950, was followed by a host of other repressive legislation. Millions of black South Africans were forcibly removed from their homes and forced to carry passes and those who opposed these injustices were subjected to banning orders, arrest, torture, and detention without trial. Few white South Africans protested; even fewer Afrikaners. But Bram and Molly Fischer did. It was important to Bram that, as an Afrikaner, he oppose apartheid. As he declared in his statement from the dock:

> [Apartheid] demands also that Afrikaners themselves should protest openly and clearly against discrimination. Surely, in such circumstances, there was an additional duty cast on me, that at least one Afrikaner should make this protest actively and positively.[4]

On 11 July 1963 the police raided Liliesleaf Farm in Rivonia, which was used secretly by senior members of the African National Congress (ANC) to plan the overthrow of the apartheid government. Among the key ANC and Communist Party leaders arrested that day were Denis Goldberg and Walter Sisulu (Nelson Mandela was already serving a five-year sentence for leaving the country without a passport and inciting workers to strike). They also found numerous documents that would become key exhibits in what became known as the Rivonia Trial.

Bram Fischer was initially reluctant to join the defence team because he was concerned that he might be implicated because he had been at Liliesleaf on various occasions and thought he might be recognised by members of the staff. But, as Mandela noted many years later:

> Joel Joffe, our attorney, and Arthur Chaskalson and George Bizos, our counsel, assumed that he would lead the defence. They put tremendous

pressure on him by using the argument that there was no other advocate in the country who could say that we had done nothing more than what his people the Afrikaners had done in 1914, and that despite the loss of life in that rebellion, there were no death sentences; that if people were to die there would never be reconciliation between black and white in South Africa.[5]

The Rivonia story and Nelson Mandela's statement from the dock are well known. The accused were spared the death sentence, in large part thanks to Bram Fischer. The day after being sentenced to life imprisonment, Nelson Mandela, Ahmed Kathrada, Walter Sisulu, Govan Mbeki, Raymond Mahlaba, Elias Motsoaledi and Andrew Mlangeni arrived on Robben Island. The sole white defendant in the trial, Denis Goldberg, was imprisoned in Pretoria.

Whatever relief Bram Fischer might have felt at the conclusion of the trial was shattered by a devastating tragedy. On 13 June 1964, while travelling to Cape Town, Bram swerved to avoid a cow in the road. The car plunged into the Sand River. Bram managed to free himself, but Molly was killed.

On 23 September 1964 Bram was arrested and charged under the Sabotage Act. After he was released on bail he requested permission to leave the country to argue a case in London. He gave his word that he would return. South Africa, he said, was his home. He was granted permission and left in October 1964, returning the following month. But in January 1965 there was a dramatic development: Fischer skipped bail and went underground. In a letter he sent to Harold Hanson, his legal counsel, he stated:

My decision was made only because I believe that it is the duty of every true opponent of this Government to remain in this country and to oppose its monstrous policy of apartheid with every means in his power. That is what I shall do for as long as I can ... If by my fight I can encourage even some people to think about, to understand and to abandon the policies they now so blindly follow, I shall not regret any punishment I may incur ... I can no longer serve justice in the way I have attempted to do during the past thirty years. I can do it only in the way I have now chosen.[6]

In his absence, Fischer was struck off the Roll of Advocates, an action that hurt him deeply. After months underground he was rearrested on 11 November 1965. He chose not to testify, instead delivering a statement from the dock. It is an eloquent and moving explanation of his reasons for opposing apartheid.

On 4 May 1966 he was convicted and two days later he was sentenced to life imprisonment. Because he was a white political prisoner he was imprisoned in Pretoria, where he was reunited with Denis Goldberg.

Decades later Fischer's family would testify to the Truth and Reconciliation Commission about the harsh and malicious treatment meted out to him. He was singled out by warders who reviled him as a traitor. When his son, Paul, passed away on 27 January 1971 he was refused permission to attend the funeral. In November 1974 he fell and broke his leg, but was not admitted to hospital for 13 days. When he returned to prison his condition had deteriorated and his fellow prisoners had to take care of him. By December, now diagnosed with cancer, he fell into a coma. Despite national and international pleas for his release, the apartheid state refused to consider it. Eventually, in March 1975, they relented. Although he was released into his brother's care, in Bloemfontein, he was still a prisoner. There would be no compassion from the apartheid state for the man they saw as a traitor.

Bram Fischer died on 8 May 1975. His family was granted permission to hold a funeral, but his ashes were confiscated and never returned. After his death, the Afrikaans-language press lamented the tragedy of his life – a theme they continue to pursue. To them, he was the golden son who turned his back on 'his' people; the man who could have ascended to the highest positions in Afrikaner society but 'threw it all away' to become a communist. That is not how Fischer or the majority of South Africans saw (and still see) it. Bram Fischer saw his allegiance as being to *all* South Africans. In his statement from the dock he declared:

> I owed it to the political prisoners, to the banished, to the silenced and to those under house arrest not to remain a spectator, but to act. I knew what they expected of me, and I did it. I felt responsible, not to those who are indifferent to the sufferings of others, but to those who are concerned. I knew that by valuing above all their judgment, I would be condemned by people who are content to see themselves as respectable and loyal citizens. I cannot regret any such condemnation that may follow me.[7]

The Afterlife of Bram Fischer

Fischer did not live to see the end of apartheid but he had a lasting effect on many of those who played prominent roles in the new South Africa. '[He] was so much braver than the rest of us, he paid so much more, his life seems to have touched the lives of so many people – even after his death', writes Antjie Krog in her widely acclaimed account of South Africa's Truth and Reconciliation Commission, *Country of My Skull*. [8] '[It] is tempting to think that … something of Bram had passed – in the best way – into history, infusing the humanising and peacemaking gestures of his being into those he left behind,' writes Stephen Clingman, whose *Bram Fischer: Afrikaner Revolutionary*, was the first significant biography of Fischer. [9]

In 1995, delivering the Legal Resources Centre's first Bram Fischer Memorial Lecture, President Mandela declared:

> In any history written of our country two Afrikaner names will be always remembered. Happily one is still with us, dear comrade Beyers Naudé. [10] The other is Bram Fischer. The people of South Africa will never forget him. He was among the first bright beacons that attracted millions of our young people to fervently believe in a non-racial democracy in our country. [11]

It is not only in South Africa that Fischer has been honoured. Since 2007 Oxford University has hosted an annual memorial lecture, initially at New College, where Fischer was once a student. The then Warden of New College, Professor Alan Ryan, played a fundamental role in establishing the lecture, which quickly outgrew the venue and is now held at

Rhodes House, a place where Bram Fischer attended many dinners as a Rhodes Scholar. The first lecture was delivered by Lord Joel Joffe, a member of the Rivonia defence team. George Bizos and Denis Goldberg have also been speakers.

One attempt to honour Bram Fischer, however, caused outrage among some Afrikaners and the Afrikaans-language media. In September 2004 it was announced that Stellenbosch University (SU) would award Fischer a posthumous honorary degree. SU, known as the 'intellectual home of apartheid', produced the presidents and prime ministers, the bureaucrats and the theologians who dreamt up, enforced and justified apartheid. The honorary degree decision, which looked like a promising attempt to acknowledge past injustice, revealed that many Afrikaners deeply resented the new non-racial South Africa.

The DPhil (*honoris causa*) was awarded by the Faculty of Arts (now Social Sciences), since the Faculty of Law refused to have any association with Bram Fischer. The Afrikaans press condemned Fischer as a bloodthirsty communist who would have murdered Afrikaners in their beds and claimed he had supported genocide. Various Afrikaner organisations followed suit in attacking Fischer. The 'Rooi Gevaar' (Red Peril) was resurrected with great gusto, serving as a thinly disguised 'Swart Gevaar' (Black Peril), used to vent fury against the new South Africa.

The SU Convocation (overwhelmingly white and male) demanded that the degree be rescinded. The SU management wavered and conceded the convocation's claim that Fischer – a champion of non-racialism – was not a role model. It was an appalling indictment of the Afrikaner community's supposed commitment to the new South Africa. For many, Fischer's commitment to non-racialism was still seen as a betrayal; he was still a 'volksverraaier'.[12]

The so-called 'Fischer debate' revealed that many white South Africans had failed to understand the moral imperative of both non-racialism and reconciliation. It 'outed' a number of Afrikaner leaders as reactionaries and heralded the start of a deeply troubling 'post-reconciliation' era in which apartheid apologias have become acceptable in the mainstream Afrikaans media.

But why this outpouring of vitriol against Bram Fischer? The reason is probably not his communism but the fact that he makes many Afrikaner elders – self-appointed and otherwise – deeply uncomfortable. Fischer could have led a very comfortable life, arguing that he would change the system 'from within', the excuse many supposedly enlightened Afrikaners used to justify their failure to oppose apartheid. But he chose a very different, very courageous route. His personal and moral stature in committing himself to justice for all South Africans is what his detractors cannot bear. They have to demonise him so that they cannot be measured against him. More than 40 years after his death Bram Fischer is still 'ahead of his time'. He remains not only an example of moral courage, but also of open-ended identity.

The Theory and Practice of Moral Courage

We do not celebrate moral courage enough. We confuse superficial celebrity with character, we mistake physical prowess for courage. Often, we do not recognise moral courage until long after the fact. And not merely because moral heroes act while others waver. More often than not, we refuse to recognise moral heroes because their courage shines a light on our own cowardice or our society's failings.

True moral courage is not an impulsive act, it is deliberate and sustained. It is a choice made despite the odds. Historian Timothy Snyder writes about those who rescued Jews during the Holocaust:

> Wanting to help was not enough. To rescue a Jew in these conditions, where no structure supported the effort and where the penalty was death, *required something stronger than character, something greater than a worldview* … It was an era when to be good meant not only the avoidance of evil but a total determination to act on behalf of a stranger, on a planet where hell, not heaven, was the reward for goodness [my emphasis].[13]

It has been said that the arc of the moral universe is long, but that it bends toward justice. Perhaps. But if it does, it is not the result of natural momentum or preordained destiny. It does not just happen. It happens because of people like Bram Fischer.

Bram Fischer could not single-handedly end apartheid. But he did what was within his power, knowing full well what the consequences might be. After the National Party came to power, after the Suppression of Communism Act and other draconian legislation became law, he continued. After his comrades were handed life sentences he did not waver. His courage was deliberate and sustained. Like many truly courageous people he paid a very high price. But his death did not cancel out his legacy nor did it extinguish the light he shone during very dark days.

We know the meaning of courage because of people like Bram Fischer. They stood for justice when the consequences might be fatal. So, however dark and dangerous the world becomes, we cannot say there were none who had the courage to spark a light, to lead the way. For the rest of us, the beneficiaries of their courage, the best we can do is to live lives worthy of such courage and sacrifice.

Conclusion

> Nikolai Ostrovsky's eulogy for a communist comrade in his 1930s novel, *How the Steel was Tempered,* could have been written for Bram: 'Man's dearest possession is life. It is given to him but once, and he must live it so as to feel no torturing regrets for wasted years, never know the burning shame of a mean and petty past; so live that dying he might say: all my life, all my strength were given to the finest cause in all the world – the fight for the Liberation of Mankind.'
>
> **Denis Goldberg**[14]

The greatest beneficiaries of Bram Fischer's courage are people who never met him: young South Africans. For his courage made the future possible. The schoolchildren and students of diverse racial backgrounds who attended *The Bram Fischer Waltz* as part of the Mangaung Metropolitan Council's Bram Fischer Week in 2015 would not have been able to be in same room had it not been for people like Fischer. He stood for a future that could barely be imagined when he died. As Clingman observes:

> [F]or Bram, understanding that the future was both known and unknown, he had staked his all on creating it, in fulfilment of the imperative to make humanity meaningful and available to everyone. That was the existential component of his commitment, the moral dimension of his

politics, the integrity in his ideology, and he had followed wherever it led. That he could do so with such conviction and courage still create a sense of mystery, as we look on across our own time and distance.[15]

South Africa has a deeply troubled past and an uncertain future, but the nation has produced moral heroes who show us the way. President Mandela noted that an unintended consequence of the oppression and brutality of apartheid was that it 'produced the Oliver Tambos, the Walter Sisulus, the Chief Luthulis, the Yusuf Dadoos, the Bram Fischers, the Robert Sobukwes of our time – men of such extraordinary courage, wisdom and generosity that their like may never be known again.'[16]

Notes

1. Zygmunt Bauman, *Modernity and the Holocaust*, p 207.
2. Stephen Clingman, *Bram Fischer: Afrikaner Revolutionary*, p 64.
3. Nelson Mandela, Bram Fischer Memorial Lecture.
4. Bram Fischer, Statement from the Dock, paragraph 64.
5. Mandela, Bram Fischer Memorial Lecture.
6. Fischer, Letter to Harold Hanson.
7. Fischer, Statement from the Dock, paragraph 65.
8. Antjie Krog, *Country of My Skull*, p 203.
9. Clingman, p 412.
10. Beyers Naude passed away on 7 September 2004.
11. Mandela, Bram Fischer Memorial Lecture.
12. Despite the outrage, the honorary degree was awarded on 9 December 2004. This was because the

proper procedure had been followed, leaving no legal or formal loophole for the degree to be rescinded.

13. Timothy Snyder, 'The Banality of Good'.

14. Denis Goldberg, Bram Fischer Memorial Lecture.

15. Clingman, p 408.

16. Mandela, Bram Fischer Memorial Lecture.

Bibliography

Bauman, Zygmunt, *Modernity and the Holocaust* (New York: Cornell University Press, 1992).

Clingman, Stephen, *Bram Fischer: Afrikaner Revolutionary* (Johannesburg: Jacana Media, 2013).

Fischer, Bram, Letter to Harold Hanson, January 1965 (Bram Fischer Archive, Bodleian Library, Oxford University).

Fischer, Bram, Statement from the Dock (copy in author's possession).

Goldberg, Denis, Bram Fischer Memorial Lecture, delivered on 27 February 2014, Oxford University.

Jacoway, Elizabeth, *Turn Away Thy Son: Little Rock, the Crisis that Shocked the Nation* (Fayetteville: The University of Arkansas Press, 2008).

Kathrada, Ahmed, *Memoirs* (Cape Town: Zebra Press, 2004).

Krog, Antjie, *Country of My Skull* (Cape Town: Random House, 1998).

Mandela, Nelson, Bram Fischer Memorial Lecture, organised by the Legal Resources Centre, delivered on 9 June 1995, Johannesburg. Available at: http://www.anc.org.za/content/first-bram-fischer-memorial-lecture-delivered-president-nelson-r-mandela

Snyder, Timothy, 'The Banality of Good', Slate.com, 8 October 2015. Available at: www.slate.com/articles/ life/history/2015/10/why_people_who_rescued_jews_ during_the_holocaust_viewed_their_heroism_as.html

Printed and bound by CPI Group (UK) Ltd, Croydon, CR0 4YY

14/04/2025

14656908-0001